Stories, sayings, and scriptures to Encourage and Inspire

hugs™

to

Comfort

Stories by
JOHN WILLIAM SMITH

Messages by
GARY MYERS

Personalized Scriptures by
LEANN WEISS

HOWARD BOOKS
A DIVISION OF SIMON & SCHUSTER
New York   London   Toronto   Sydney

Our Purpose at Howard Books is to:
 • *Increase* faith in the hearts of growing Christians
 • *Inspire* holiness in the lives of believers
 • *Instill* hope in the hearts of struggling people everywhere
Because He's coming again!

HOWARD
BOOKS

Published by Howard Books, a division of Simon & Schuster, Inc.
1230 Avenue of the Americas, New York, NY 10020
www.howardpublishing.com

Hugs to Comfort © 2007 Stories by John William Smith

Library of Congress Cataloging-in-Publication Data

Smith, John William, 1937-
    Hugs to comfort : stories, sayings, and scriptures to encourage and inspire / [stories by John William Smith ; inspirational messages by G.A. Myers ; edited by Philis Boultinghouse].
        p. cm
                    13 Digit ISBN: 978-1-4516-5522-3

    1. Consolation. I. Myers, G. A., 1955- II. Boultinghouse, Philis, 1951- III. Title.

    BV4905.3.S635 2007
    242—dc22
                                                    2006043671

10 9 8 7 6 5 4 3 2 1

HOWARD colophon is a registered trademark of Simon & Schuster, Inc.

Manufactured in the United States of America

For information regarding special discounts for bulk purchases, please contact Simon & Schuster Special Sales at 1-800-456-6798 or business@simonandschuster.com.

Edited by Philis Boultinghouse
Inspirational messages by G. A. Myers
Cover design by John Mark Luke Designs
Interior design by John Mark Luke Designs

Paraphrased scriptures © 2007 LeAnn Weiss, 3006 Brandywine Drive, Orlando, FL 32806; 407-898-4410

Scriptures taken from the *Holy Bible, New International Version*®. Copyright© 1973, 1978, 1984 by International Bible Society. Used by permission of Zondervan. All rights reserved.

Contents

The Gift of

Rest

Life can be tiring and frustrating at times!
Come to me when you are worn down —
stressed out with circumstances and
burdens that are weighing you down.
I will give you rest!

Love,
Your God of Peace and Rest

—FROM MATTHEW 11:28-30

3

Do you ever feel that your life is a horrible nightmare? Do you sometimes wish you could just wake up and it would all go away?

When the haze of pain threatens to shut out all the light in your life, it's time to gaze at the eternal light far off in the distance. This inviting light offers comfort, peace, and an enduring hope that no darkness can smother. This light is the light of home – your real home. It's the light of heaven. When life becomes a bad dream, close your eyes and take a little mind trip to heaven – it's a wonderful place to visit.

In the last weeks of Christ's life, when the darkness of betrayal and death hovered over him, he comforted his confused followers with thoughts of heaven: "Don't let your hearts be troubled. Trust in God; trust also in me. In my Father's house are many rooms…"

Can you picture it? The

fresh fragrance of new construction fills
the place. Each room and every hallway
is lit up with the warm love of the living God.
No fear lurks in the darkness, because there is no
darkness. And listen, do you hear the music? It's
the joyful sound of angels' songs.

You approach a doorway where Jesus is standing.
With one nail-scarred hand he points to a golden
nameplate, and with the other he touches your
shoulder. The nameplate bears your name; his
gentle voice speaks words of assurance, "Take
heart. I have overcome the world and all of its
pain. One day you will be with me in this place,
and all that you are going through now will
seem only a bad dream. Until then, feel free
to visit here in your heart anytime you
wish. And by the way, you can invite
as many as you can to come with
you. There's plenty of room."

Life was born again by the morning – I tingled with it – I wanted to open the window and shake my fist at The Nameless Dread and say, "I beat you."

The Nameless Dread

When I was a child, I had a recurring bad
dream. In my dream I was standing on a vast,
flat, endless, unbroken, grassy plain. There
were no large rocks, valleys, hills, trees, water,
people, or towns – not a single place to hide
or seek shelter. I had no idea how I got to this
place – it was as though I had been suddenly
born there. As I looked about me, I was filled
with a sense of dread – as though I were in
danger from some as yet unknown source.
I slowly became aware of something like a
vast cloud bank that stretched from earth to
sky and from one edge of the horizon to the
other. It moved slowly but purposefully in my

direction, becoming darker and more ominous with each moment. It was –

The Nameless Dread!

I do not know how it got that title – it was not of my doing. I only know that from the first time I saw it, I knew –

that was its name.

My reaction was always the same. I would begin to run – to seek any kind of shelter. I ran slowly at first, casting my eyes frantically about me, sure that there must be – had to be – some nook that I had overlooked. Finding nothing, I would increase my pace as the dark horror drew nearer. Ultimately, I would find myself running in abject terror as fast as I could until I was totally exhausted – until my breath came in ragged gasps – until my legs simply would no longer move at my bidding. I would scream for help, but my screams could only be heard in my head – never in my ears – and I was aware that in this land there was no sound, because there was no one to hear. The sound went out, but it never came back.

I was alone.

Alone in a way that I had never known –
alone with
The Nameless Dread.

The Nameless Dread

The creeping darkness was cruelly relentless. It never hurried, changed its pace, or varied its direction. It was absolutely sure of its quarry. Actually, The Nameless Dread wasn't after me – I mean, personally and individually. I was nothing to it – no more than a stone or blade of grass – it simply moved across the plain every day, consuming everything in its path.

At the end of my dream, when I had reached the last extremity of my strength, I would fall to my knees, interlock my fingers, and raise my hands in a supplicating posture and beg for mercy. I would cry and plead for clemency in the most touching, sympathetic, and endearing terms. The Nameless Dread never responded. It did not and could not hear. It never altered its countenance

– it simply came on.

Just as it reached me – just as I was about to be enveloped and overwhelmed by its misty blackness, which I always interpreted as death, I awoke. My first waking sensation was always the vague awareness of light. I would gradually, fearfully open my eyes – assuming that I was dead and wondering what kind of world I was waking to – and the light would grow. Familiar things – the quilt, the picture on the wall, my chest of drawers – came into view. I would look out the window and there would be the chicken coop – right where it ought to be – the well and the pump, the outhouse, the pear tree, and then, down below the house, the misty fog rising from the swamp. I was alive! It had only been a dream.

"Oh God," I would say, "Oh God,

it was just a dream –

it was just a dream –

it was just a dream!"

Over and over I would repeat that phrase as the wonderful, dawning reality swept over me that I was not dead – that I was not awakening to a new and frightening world. I would be drenched with sweat, trembling from head to foot; real tears would streak my face, and my fingers would ache from being clenched for so long. Gradually, I would begin to relax, pulling the familiar quilt up around my chin – its realness assuring me – as the glory of being alive – of living – washed over me.

You cannot imagine the pleasure I took in the simplest things. I would slowly finger my old, worn blanket – made for me by my grandma Smith – tracing the quilted pattern as

though I were seeing it for the first time. The chicken coop and the outhouse were not the drab, decaying, ordinary things they had been. They were wonderful, glorious structures – and I took individual pleasure in them. The smells from our kitchen would float into my room, and they were not of ham and eggs but of exotic dishes – ambrosia and the nectar of the gods. All of these things were created anew for me every time I had the dream. Life was born again by the morning – I tingled with it – I wanted to open the window and shake my fist at

The Nameless Dread

and say,

"I beat you."

All of us at times feel the creeping, overwhelming, blackness of The Nameless Dread. It has many names and many faces, and it comes in many forms. We call it aging or loneliness or cancer. We call it fear, heartache, hopelessness, ingratitude, guilt, death, or depression. And when it enters our lives, we run before it, frantically seeking shelter, vainly seeking help.

And finally, we reach the last extremity of our strength, and we fall to our knees, begging for clemency – and we

lift our eyes to heaven – and we see standing there God, the Father, with arms outstretched, with comfort in His eyes. He's standing where he's always been – waiting for us to look up – waiting for us to seek his aid.

Deliverance from The Nameless Dread does not necessarily mean deliverance from its earthly forms – for we are not promised relief from aging, from heartache, from sickness, or from death – but we are offered relief from the hopelessness of it all, relief from the feelings of powerlessness, relief from the dread of it all. We are offered hope and joy even in the midst of pain.

And even greater than the relief we find here is the absolute relief on the other side of the sleep of death. For when children of God awake, the next sensation will be of light. We will open our eyes to familiar objects and familiar faces. "Yes," we'll say, "there is the pear tree and there is the chicken coop and there are my loved ones – Jary, Priscilla, Mom and Dad, Judi, Lincoln, Amy, Brendan, Kamber, Kristen, and Debbie. And there is the Holy City – just as John described it and more glorious than I ever imagined it." The alabaster walls reach ever higher, and at the twelve gates, each made of a single

pearl, stands a herald to welcome the children of God. The city stands sparkling in the brilliant light – but it's not the sun – this light is truer, cleaner, whiter, and clearer than ever the sun knew. There are no shadows here, for the light is everywhere – it is the light of presence – of being – of God's own face beaming in the glorious victory of His Son.

"*Oh God,*" we will say, "Oh God" – and it won't be a word of hope but of reality.

"Oh God, it was just a dream,

it was just a dream,

and now I am alive –

more alive than I have ever been –

and I shall never sleep again

and never, never again fear –

The Nameless Dread."

reflections . . .

Chapter 2

The Gift of *Life*

You can soar even in storms because I strengthen you! Remember, you can do all things through me!

Love,

Your Father of Every Good and Perfect Gift

P.S. I have given you everything you need for life and godliness

—FROM PHILIPPIANS 4:13; 2 PETER 1:3

You have been given a gift. This gift is not wrapped in tissue paper or tied with a beautiful bow, but it has been prepared with the greatest of care by the Master Gift Giver. Priceless in nature, no gift in all the world is more sought after than this – it is the gift of life – your life.

And yet, even before this gift was yours, it was tainted by the schemes of the Spoiler – for his intent is to spoil all that's good. He sends rains of sorrow and floods of defeat, but the Gift Giver will not have his purposes thwarted. For through the storms of life, the Savior's voice is heard more clearly than before, and

his presence is felt with intense reality.
Through blinding rain, the Life Giver
extends his nail-scarred hand and takes your
trembling hand firmly in his own.

With our hands safe in his, we borrow what
we need from him. He lends us his courage and
strength, and paths that we thought were impassable
pass beneath our feet, and we move with him beyond
the storm. And there, in the gleaming light of
day, we see the eternal value of our lives and
know that the gift of life here on earth is
made even more valuable by virtue of the
chastening of the storm.

Your life is a gift.

God may be *invisible*, but He's in touch.
You may not be able to see *Him*, but
He is in *control*. And that includes
what you've just lost. That *includes*
what you've just *gained*. That includes
all of life——past, present, future.

—*Charles R. Swindoll*

"Just follow me, and do what I do. I always save a little for the end — for this last hill — you can borrow from me."

The Life of Susan Edgin

She was the older sister of my son's wife, and her name was Susan. She was a nice girl – a good girl. She was good in the traditional sense that she loved her family, her friends, her dog, obeyed her parents, studied hard, slept late, was kind and thoughtful of others, sang in the church choir, cleaned up her messes, made good moral decisions, loved God, was silly, laughed a lot, cried some, and all in all, was the kind of daughter every parent dreams of having. She loved life and lived it to the fullest every waking moment. She took good care of her body, watched what she ate, exercised regularly, was neat in her appearance, and went to great pains with her hair and clothes.

The Gift of *Life*

I think that at first glance she would be judged as no more than average-pretty, but if you looked deeply into those large, luminous, all-telling eyes or listened attentively to that intriguing, animated voice, it would soon occur to you that she was quite beautiful. She was a tall girl, lithe, athletic, and graceful in all her movements. She carried herself well – with dignity, style, and verve. She never took herself too seriously, but she was thoughtful enough to be introspective when the occasion called for it. She was a loyal friend, a great lover of children and simple things of life, and she sang beautifully.

I know you think that I am just romanticizing, but I'm not. My son put it this way: "If you went anywhere I have ever lived, you would find someone who didn't like me, but that wasn't true of Susan. I never met or heard of anyone who didn't like Susan Edgin."

For the short time I knew her, we spent a fair amount of time together. Susan was so refreshingly open that you didn't need to be around her long to feel that you were her best friend.

Once, when I was staying at her house, we went running together. She thoughtfully adjusted her pace to

accommodate my aging legs. Susan talked the whole way. (I am tempted to make a pun and say she kept up a running conversation, but I won't.) I don't talk when I run. It isn't that I am concentrating or unfriendly; it's that talking requires breath and energy, and I don't have any to spare when I'm running. After about four miles, I was nearing exhaustion. We came at last to the bottom of the long, steep hill that led to her house.

As we approached the incline, I said, "Susan, I just can't make it; you go ahead."

"Sure you can," she said, "just follow me, and do what I do. I always save a little for the end – for this last hill – you can borrow from me."

I followed her.

I did what she did,

and I borrowed a little

of what she had saved

for the end.

When we got to the top, she turned and laughed and said, "See there, you can always do a little more than you think –

especially if you have someone with you."

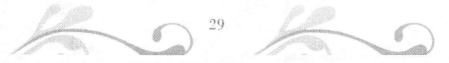

The Gift of *Life*

Susan's gone now. She died on May 19, 1995, in an automobile accident near Augusta, Georgia. The car she was traveling in spun out of control on a wet road and slammed sideways into a guardrail. Susan was crushed. In the short time she lived after the accident, calls went out for prayers. We poured out our hearts to God in agony, begging him to save her. The doctors tried everything that medical science could do, but she died.

It doesn't seem fair, you know. Here I am still plodding up hills, and I'm thirty-five years older than Susan – it doesn't seem right. You can't help the nagging doubts; they are an integral part of a growing faith. I started asking those questions a long time ago. The only answer I've found is to trust God. It hasn't been easy, and I still ask the questions, but I know that I don't have a clue – so I trust him.

What is life?

I think I know. Life is a gift – a precious, beautiful, gift. Yes, that is exactly what life is. It is something to hold – but not too closely – because it isn't ours. God gave Susan to us for twenty-seven years, and he let us know her and love her and bask in the glow of her vitality – but

she was never ours. That is the great mistake we make. We become so used to things that we begin to think they're ours. That's what leads us into asking stupid questions about justice and fairness and –

"What if . . . ?"

Even our personal lives are not our own. Life has nothing to do with fairness, and its value or justification cannot be measured by longevity. It is not sad to die young. What is sad is to die and never to have lived, to have been alive and never to have seen anything or known God. We don't feel that kind of sadness for Susan. Susan lived a full life because she saw the created world through the eyes of faith and because she knew the God who made it.

Susan was a gift – and the only proper response to a gift – is gratitude.

"Thank you,
O Lord of the Universe,
for Susan."

I honestly don't remember the last time I saw her or what we said. We didn't try to make it important because we thought we'd see each other again – soon and often. I guess it really wasn't too important, because we will see

The Gift of _Life_

each other again – soon and often – and we'll pick up right where we left off.

Susan has climbed her last hill – it was a long, steep grade – even for young legs, and she didn't know if she could make it, but when she started the ascent, she found Jesus beside her, and he said –

"Just follow me, and do what I do.

I always save a little for the end –

for this last hill –

you can borrow from me."

And so she followed Jesus, and she did what he did, and she borrowed some of what he had saved, and they climbed the hill together and passed over to the other side. And it's true, you know –

it is easier

if you have someone with you.

Life is a gift.

reflections . . .

Chapter

3

The Gift of

Healing

*Your flesh and your heart may fail.
But, remember . . . I am the strength
of your heart and your destiny forever!*

Love,

*Your God of Healing
and Restoration*

——FROM PSALM 73:26

$\mathcal{O}ur$ God is a God of healing. He is a mender, a fixer of broken things. And we need such a God, because we tend to break and spoil much of what we touch. When we allow him to come into our fretful hearts, he works quietly and gently; and with the skill of a tender craftsman, he begins the work of restoring what is lost.

You won't feel his every move, but one day you'll sense a change – a change that stirs within you the desire to right a wrong. Perhaps you'll be moved

to write a letter to a friend or relative
who has been distanced by anger or bitter-
ness. Perhaps you'll think of calling a cherished
loved one whom you hurt with careless words.

Go on, make the move. You'll find that God has
already prepared the path to restored love. It may
not be easy at first – mending broken hearts never
is – but the Miracle Maker has already applied his
providence and touched the heart awaiting your
move.

Always be in a state of *expectancy*,
and see that you *leave* room for
God to come in as *He* likes.

—*Oswald Chambers*

For the first time in a long time,

he had a plan — he knew exactly

what he was doing and why.

Going Home

If you asked him why he came back, he would
have said that, quite honestly, he didn't know.
He had been born here and had graduated from
high school here and married here. He had
grown up in this town. He had played football
here and, after four years of college, had returned
here to marry his high-school sweetheart. He
hadn't been back in years. It wasn't that he had
no good memories. It was that
the latest and most dominant were bad.

Lately, he had just felt a great wrongness
in his life. An undefined anxiety – depression
– heaviness. He found himself sitting at his
desk drumming his fingers and staring vacantly

at reports wondering why they were important. Sometimes he turned the nameplate that sat on the front of his desk around and stared at his name – "George Franklin," he said. "Who is George Franklin?" He gazed long moments out his office window at the windows in other office buildings, wondering who worked over there and what they were like. He wondered what they thought about and if they ever looked at his window and wondered about him. He also noticed, with some alarm, that he was having trouble making even the most simple decisions.

He knew he was lonely, but this maddening, haunting feeling nothing seemed to shake was more than loneliness – it was like the instinct that drives a wounded animal to its den. He felt the need to *get somewhere* – someplace where he could find his center again, his foundation – his *home*. Yes, that was exactly what he wanted, and that was why he had come back to this town – it was the closest thing to home he had ever known.

This primitive instinct drives many thoughtful people – it drives some to drink, some to drugs, some to work harder, some to power, some to affairs, some to church,

Going Home

some to diets, travel, poetry, mysticism, fitness centers, sporting events, TV, or cheap novels.

It drove him

home.

When he drove into town, he was very disappointed. Much was gone; much more had changed. He didn't recognize anyone. Now that he was here, he didn't know what to do. He had thought that just coming back would provide the reason – it didn't. He drove around a little – went by the high school, looking for old, familiar land- marks. He stopped in a restaurant for a cup of coffee and finally recognized an old acquaintance. They shook hands, exchanged pleasantries, and bragged a little on what they had accomplished. "How's Alice?" Pete asked. It was an inevitable question, but it was the one he wanted to avoid the most of all. "She's fine, I guess. I suppose you haven't heard that we're separated. I haven't seen her in nearly two years."

"Separated! No kidding! Everybody thought you were Mr. and Mrs. Ideal Couple. Two years! Why don't you just get a divorce?"

He'd wondered the same thing – many times. He

The Gift of *Healing*

wondered why she hadn't forced the issue – demanded one. He mumbled some nonsense about the financial difficulty of the settlement; and of course, they couldn't agree about the kids – but there was something else, something more – something never put into words, but he knew what it was. Divorce was too *final – the end* – neither of them had the courage or the heart to say that it was finally and forever over. That would close the book on too many things they wanted to keep.

Pete was in the real-estate business, and finally George asked him if he remembered the house they had lived in. "Sure," Pete said. "In fact, I've got it listed." Without really thinking about it, George said, "Let's drive by; I'd like to see what they've done to the old place."

His mind flooded with memories as they drove down the familiar street – maybe he had been happier here than he thought. Pete had a key to the lockbox, and very shortly, George found himself wandering through the empty rooms. *This is it*, he said to himself; *this is why I came back.*

And he knew the truth.

Going Home

The grass had not been cut in back. The previous own-ers had not cared properly for the grapes or the fruit trees; the bedrooms were badly in need of paint. *You know,* he thought, *I always meant to pipe the water from the washing machine out to the trees, and I think Alice was right about putting a mantel over the fireplace. In fact, now that Scott is bigger, we could finish that back room, put in another bath, and have a bedroom to ourselves.*

It began to dawn upon him – very slowly – what a good time he was having, how excited he was, that he was planning in terms of *we* instead of *I* – and that gave meaning to the future. But his excitement vanished as he realized it was all a myth, a cruel unreality. It struck him forcefully that he didn't own this house, he didn't live in this town, he had no job here, and of course, Alice and the kids lived far away. But the idea wouldn't leave him, and he knew – just as a homing pigeon knows – that he was home and *this was his one chance* and that

he had to try.

"How much are they asking, Pete?"

The Gift of *Healing*

"One hundred fifty thousand, but they'll take one twenty."

"I'll take it." George couldn't believe it was his voice that he heard. There was assurance in it. For the first time in a long time, *he had a plan* – he knew exactly what he was doing and why. *I'll call her*, he thought; *I'll call her tonight*. But he couldn't wait for tonight, so he called her at work. Normally he asked for "Alice," but today he asked for "Mrs. George Franklin." He heard the secretary whisper, "Alice, it's for you, some guy wants to speak to Mrs. *George Franklin*." When she picked up the phone, her first words were, "George, I hope this is you. I've been thinking about you all day."

"Alice, I just bought the old house back. Could we get together this weekend and talk? It's important to me."

"I just happen to be free this weekend, and I don't know anybody I'd rather spend it with than you."

They met.

Love mended.

She stayed.

Forever.

Going Home

A noble impulse acted upon reunited two people who had allowed the petty things of life to drive them apart. George and Alice Franklin mended their broken relationship and began rebuilding their life together.

Are you burdened with a heavy sense of wrongness? Do you find yourself looking out your window and into other people's? Have you lost touch with the important people in your life?

God's providential touch may already be working to help you rebuild broken relationships.

Do you need to call somebody?

reflections . . .

The Gift of

Hope

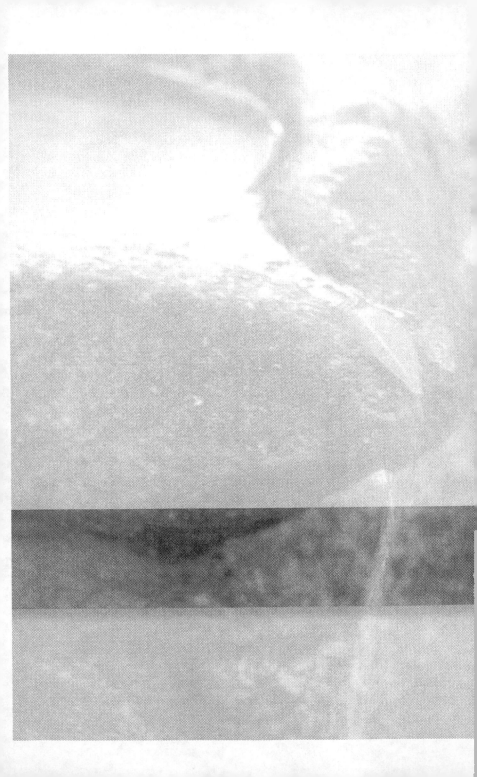

I love you, and by my amazing grace,
I give you never-ending encouragement
and good hope. I'm working behind the
scenes to encourage your heart and to
strengthen you in every good deed and word.

Love,

Your God of All Hope

—FROM 2 THESSALONIANS 2:16–17

Something is wrong – a regrettable something . . . a heartbreaking something . . . an unexpected and unnerving something. You can't seem to rid yourself of its darkening effect. You've tried to drown it out, drive it away, and push it aside. But it's still with you. Something is wrong.

But there's a solution. There is some*one* right for your some*thing* wrong. He's a healer with a gentle touch, a sympathetic smile, and an intense love. When he speaks, you'll want to listen; when you speak, he hears with an attentive heart. When you see him, you'll notice that he bears deep scars on his hands, his feet, his head, and his side – from a time when things went desperately wrong for him.

In fact, the first things he will want to tell you about are those brutal reminders of something gone wrong.

Don't turn away.

Those ugly mortal wounds hold wonderfully good news for you. They are the key to a *peace* that surpasses pain, to a *confidence* that dispels confusion, to a *hope* that replaces heartbreak.

Run to him, and fall into his embrace.

Jesus has been expecting you – for about 2000 years.

Hope is like the *sun*, which, as we *journey* toward it, casts the shadow of our *burden* behind us.

—Samuel Smiles

"Oh God," he murmured audibly, "help me." And God did.

Something's Wrong

·

It all began because he forgot to turn his car radio on. Those who believe in that sort of thing would call it *providential*, but he did not believe in that sort of thing and would have dismissed it as *circumstantial*.

His wife, Carol, had turned the radio off the evening before because it was news time and her life was depressing enough without the news. Vic always listened to the radio. It was a thirty-minute commute to work, and he passed the time by tapping his fingers on the steering wheel, mouthing a few words, and occasionally even trying to imitate the lead singer. But today — at 6:15 a.m. — he simply forgot to turn it on and consequently fell into an unaccustomed pattern of subconscious thought. Out of that jumbled maze of conflicting future plans and dissatisfaction with past and present ones, a synthesis began to arise. Like a giant air bubble escaping from deep beneath the floor of the ocean where it has lain trapped for centuries, a thought rose with ever-increasing speed and burst upon the surface of his consciousness –

something is wrong.

The words were clear, unmistakable. But then they dissipated, leaving only a nagging irritation, like when you don't feel good, but you aren't exactly sick. He reached over quickly and snapped on the radio – reflexive defense against such unwelcome intrusions – and the thought was lost in the familiar rhythms and lyrics. Well, not exactly lost, but it didn't bother him for many days.

The next time it happened was due to another rare "circumstantial" occurrence. It was the kind of thing that doesn't happen often, but when it does, it is perfectly believable, and the story is told and retold. Only a *very* religious person would have called it providence, and he wasn't even mildly religious. This time, he and Carol had gone to some friends' house for dinner. They were late arriving, and in the hurry and confusion of carrying in the salad and some rolls Carol made, Vic *accidentally* hit his automatic door lock and locked both his keys and Carol's purse in the car. Their friends had one car in the shop and the other loaned out to a teenage son. Since his house was less than a mile away, Vic decided just to walk home and get his extra set of keys.

A mile is a lot farther than you think when you're alone and it's quiet. There really isn't much to do but think, and he hadn't gone far when the process began. He recognized it, and made several evasive mental moves to block its progress. He walked faster – he concentrated on logistic problems at work – he planned a vacation – but always, behind every maneuver, the process accelerated toward its conclusion. He wished desperately for his telephone, television, radio, even a book or secretary, but nothing came to his aid. He couldn't hold it down. It absolutely burst into consciousness –

Something is wrong!

And of course something was; in fact, nearly everything was. His job was dissatisfying, yet very demanding. He

The Gift of *Hope*

owed a large amount of money. His marriage was superficial and based more on convenience than love. He had little interest in his children, and they had even less in him. Nothing seemed to taste good anymore, and his laughter was mechanical and heavy. He felt empty – without hope. And one other thing – underneath it all – were those eternal *whys?* His response to the nagging questions had been evasion and philosophy – both of which left him empty and dissatisfied.

He was frantic.

Like the first escaping bubble, so the next thought rose unbidden from so deep within that he could not have identified the place, and the source was totally beyond his reckoning. "Oh God," he murmured audibly, "help me."

And God did.

By *God*, he didn't mean that well-defined, infinite, fully revealed, divine personality known and understood by those whose faith has matured. He only knew that his problems and questions were greater than himself, and so he used a colloquialism that he had learned both from his childhood and his culture. But that great, eternal Spirit, who in the beginning moved upon the

64

face of the waters and who hovers ever near us, waiting for even the slightest opening, dispatched a messenger to respond.

The message was conveyed to a fellow employee in Vic's department – an underling actually, a rather unobtrusive man whom Vic knew only slightly but whom he had always regarded with some degree of sympathetic disdain because of his lack of drive and business acumen. This employee put a note on Vic's desk two days later, inviting him to a men's Bible study and discussion group at his home. Normally, Vic would have smiled condescendingly and discarded the note. But this time he put it in his pocket, and when the evening came, he went. He was never the same –

and he was glad.

You may not be totally without faith, as Vic was, but you may be haunted by feelings of hopelessness and uncertainty. God is working in your life too. His Spirit hovers, ever near, bidding you to seek his comfort. The process of healing will take some time, but you can be confident that hope and assurance are found in him. Open yourself up to his healing and comfort –

and you'll be glad.

reflections . . .

The Gift of
Significance

I created you fearfully and wonderfully for significance and purpose! Even before you were conceived, I planned all your days. I'm always watching over you, and I'm familiar with all your ways. Wherever you go, I guide you. My right hand securely holds your precious life.

Love,

Your God of Purpose

—FROM PSALM 139

It's a Wonderful Life, with Jimmy Stewart and Donna Reed, is a favorite of young and old alike. Why? Because its message is one we all long to hear: *your life is precious!* And it's true, you know. Your life touches the lives of others in a unique, meaningful way – in a way that no other life can. Other people in this world lean on you when they're hurting, want you by their sides when they're struggling. A pretty sizable hole would be left if you weren't around.

In the same light, there are people in this world whom *you* depend on. How about the friend who wept with you when you

faced your greatest loss? Or your mom
or dad who showed you that failure is
not final and that true love is unconditional.
Or how about the brother or sister with whom
you've shared some of your deepest secrets – and
they're still secrets.

Sometimes you might allow insecurities and other
influences to convince you that your life doesn't
matter – that you hold no special significance. But
God's love proclaims your significance! Why?
Because you're *you!* That's enough for him.

You have been given a great gift – the gift
of significance!

No one is useless to God.
No One.

—*Max Lucado*

When she hung up, there were great tears in her eyes, and she hugged me and kissed me.

Rubber Ice

It was late February or early March. James and I were playing at the gravel pit. It was a cold, windy, overcast day, but we were having a great time. I had on my first pair of genuine boots – rubber footwear that you could actually stick your foot right down into with no shoes on – and you didn't have to buckle them. They were black with red soles and a little too big for my feet. (My mother had bought them at a sale, and neither size nor comfort was a major consideration.) Even with two pairs of socks, I "clumped" considerably. They came almost to my knees and looked like firemen's boots.

I was exceedingly proud of them.

The Gift of *Significance*

There was a little thin ice at the edge of the gravel pit, and we were breaking it by stomping on it and then splashing through into the shallow water beneath. I had been doing this for some time when I found a small pool, covered with what we called "rubber ice." It was not actually part of the gravel pit, but it was connected by a narrow neck of water. The ice would actually give with your weight and then spring back – a sort of trampoline effect. You can imagine what fun I had with it. Suddenly, it gave way, and I fell into some sandy water unlike any I had ever been in before. I sank immediately over my boots up to my thighs. Terrified, I began to struggle but simply could not extricate myself. This produced a fear that resulted in an absolute frenzy of effort to get out. The only noticeable result was that I was nearly up to my armpits within a minute or so.

I did not know that I should remain calm – I simply wore myself out struggling. Finally, I had no energy left, and the absolute futility of further efforts overwhelmed me. James heard my cries and came to help me, but he quickly realized he could be of no assistance. He stood completely helpless, within ten feet of me. As I grew more

calm, I noticed that I wasn't sinking as fast. I told James to run and get Elmer Russell. He was a well driller, and I knew he was home because I had spoken to him on my way to the gravel pit.

When they returned a few minutes later, I had sunk past my armpits. I was numb from the effect of the freezing sand and water and was quite concerned about my condition. Elmer had brought a rope, and he got a circle of it over my head, and I grabbed it with my hands. Being an extremely powerful man, he pulled me out with relative ease. Unfortunately, he pulled me right out of my boots. It was about a mile or so to my house, but I ran all the way –

in my socks.

I thought I would receive the whipping of my life – but instead, the funniest thing happened. When my mother first saw me – soaking wet, mud and sand right up to my ears, my boots gone – she was real upset. I tried to tell her what had happened, but it was a less than convincing story. Just about the time I finished my explanation, the phone rang; it was Elmer Russell calling to see if I had gotten home all right. He talked to my mom –

for a long time.

The Gift of *Significance*

When she hung up, there were great tears in her eyes, and she hugged and kissed me. She helped me undress, got the washtub, heated some water, and made me take a hot bath – it wasn't even Saturday – gave me some hot tea, and put me to bed. I couldn't make any sense out of it at all. When my father came home that evening, I thought sure I was going to catch it good.

For some reason, they went to their bedroom to talk, which was really unusual, because normally when I messed up, they talked right in front of me – so I would know what was coming, I guess. I heard her say, "Oh Fred, Elmer told me that another five minutes and he would have been gone. We almost lost him." When my dad came out, he didn't say much, but I noticed when we prayed at supper that night, he mentioned me several times and told God how grateful he was that He looked after me when he couldn't.

On Sunday afternoon, he and I walked over to the gravel pit, and I showed him the place – I guess he wanted to look for my boots, but they were nowhere in sight. He stood there by the little pond of water for a long time and looked, and again, he didn't say much; but I thought I

noticed him wiping his eyes a time or two with the back of his hand, and I wondered about it, because the wind was hardly blowing –

and it wasn't that cold.

The lesson is – I know you see it – how the threat of loss makes all that we hold dear more precious – how it moves the love in our hearts. And if the threat of loss moves mere mortals to greater love, how much more does it move our heavenly Father? He sees us struggling frantically to find meaning and purpose in our lives, yet always ending in great lostness. How pleased he is to circle his great arms around us and rescue us from certain death. And when he carries us home, he says, with great concern, to Jesus and the angelic host –

"You know, we almost lost him."

P.S. Late that fall, I was playing at the gravel pit one sunny afternoon with James (I wasn't real bright as a youngster – some might argue that age hasn't helped substantially), and we found one of my boots sticking right up out of the ground. I pulled it out and took it home, but it wasn't much good. I always wondered what happened to the other one.

reflections . . .

The Gift of

Love

Even when your spirit grows faint within you,
I know the right and perfect way for you.
I'll get you safely through the hidden traps.
My endless love for you endures forever! I
promise I will never abandon you!

Love,

Your Creator and
Faithful Father

—FROM PSALMS 138:8; 142:3; DEUTERONOMY 31:6

$\mathcal{I}$ have a question for you. It's not one of those easy, multiple-choice questions, where the answer is provided and all you have to do is guess the right one. No, this is one of those harder questions – it's a fill-in-the-blank. Are you ready?

When times are tough and you feel lost in a sea of sadness, when you feel confused and uncertain of your future, what is the one thing you can absolutely, unquestionably, securely trust? _____

Of course, there are some answers that can easily be ruled out. You know you can't trust your career, money, education, possessions, or the government. When you're really hurting, these are the very things that seem to leave you and let you down the hardest. They are absolutely worthless in bringing comfort or hope. So what's left? Have you filled in the blank yet?

Let me give you a few hints: It's strong enough to move

mountains; it's gentle enough to wipe the tear from a child's cheek; it's enduring enough to withstand any crisis; it's healing enough to mend the most broken heart; it's faithful enough to stay when everything else has left or been lost.

It is love – authentic, anchored, life-altering love. It is God's love. Don't waste your time pursuing anything else. Everything else will fail you. Nothing else satisfies, heals, protects, or provides like God's love.

When you call, he comes – he promised he would. When you cry, he tastes salt – he knows your pain. When you can't get up, he lifts you – you are his passion. When you pray for his presence, don't be surprised if you hear a comforting voice in your spirit saying, "I'm already here."

Then, as you lie in the lap of his love, you can look into his eyes and say, "I knew you'd come."

The *lengths* to which this God will go to express his *love* for us are almost *beyond* belief—almost, but not quite.

—Jim McGuiggan

Travis quietly explained his need to go, and even here, in this cold, barren, forbidding setting, the commanding officer realized that there was something not to be treated with normal rules.

I Knew You'd Come

I heard this story from George Romney, then governor of Michigan, in 1955, when I was a junior in high school. It made a deep impression on me, and I have never forgotten it. It is a story about love. I have made up the names, but the rest of the story is told as I remember him telling it.

In the great Ohio Valley, where the fertile, black, loamy soil produces the wheat, corn, potatoes, and other staples for the tables of Detroit and Chicago, there is a small town called Steubenville. It is an old town. Two hundred years old – and before that – the area was settled by German immigrants who were dissatisfied with life in their native land. What they found there, they liked. They cleared their land; they built their homes; they established towns, schools, and churches; they had their families – and they stayed.

There is a very old family there named Hansen. It is said that there have always been Hansens in Steubenville. The Hansens are good citizens, close-knit, solid, dependable, courteous, loyal, and helpful. It is a great tribute to the Hansens that whenever a Hansen son or daughter is sent to school, every teacher and administrator is pleased by the prospect.

Some years ago – in the early forties, actually – Lutz Hansen and his wife, Gwendolyn, had two sons in successive years. In fact, they were born eleven months apart. The older, they named him Travis; the younger, James. They had other children – older and eventually younger – but between these two, there developed a closeness, a relationship – a tie – that even in a close-knit family was remarkable – they were inseparable.

Blond, sturdy, intelligent, both were good athletes and good students – and they were always together. They worked, played, even studied together. They were a year apart in school, but with his parents' permission

and understanding, Travis stayed out his freshman year of high school so that he and James could play sports together and graduate together. Stories are still told of the way they blocked for each other in football and passed to each other in basketball, how Travis pitched and James caught in baseball, how they always double-dated, and how the girls said it didn't matter which one you went with, because you had a feeling you were out with both of them.

Whey they graduated, it was the time of the Korean conflict. They both registered for the draft, and when inducted under the "buddy system," they went to basic training together and later were assigned to the same unit, the same company. They arrived at the Yalu River, north of Panmunjom in January, 1950, in time for a major offensive.

Normally they took their duties together, but one night, James was assigned to a routine perimeter patrol designed to prevent enemy encroachment upon their position. The patrol was ambushed, and only two members struggled back to camp to report the disaster.

James did not come back.

The Gift of *Love*

When word reached Travis, he went immediately to his commanding officer and requested permission to go and search for his brother. It was denied. The place of the ambush was assumed to be in enemy control, and it would be suicide to send a rescue squad. Travis quietly explained his need to go, and even here, in this cold, barren, forbidding setting, the commanding officer realized there was something unusual, something not to be treated with normal rules. He also realized the boy was going to go – with or without permission.

He finally said that although he could not grant permission, he would not prevent his leaving. Travis spoke to the other two men who had made it back, learned of the location of the ambush, and set out. It was completely dark; it was unbearably cold; it was a hopeless task; and even if found, his brother had little chance of being alive.

All through that dark night he searched, and just at gray light, he located the place. He moved quickly from one frozen, shattered body to another – not him – not him – and then he found him, nearly frozen, mortally wounded, but alive. He cradled the head of his dying brother in his lap and wept. James opened unseeing eyes, and with the last of his strength whispered –

"Is that you, Travis?"

"Yes."

"I knew you'd come –
I've been waiting."

It was the last thing he said. A short time later, he died.

Do things like that really happen? Does love that strong really exist? When Governor Romney told the story, I believed it with all my heart. I want badly to believe it now. Sometimes I need something like this to restore my faith in man's power to do good.

James trusted his brother because of the love between them, because love always produces a covenant of trust. He waited because he knew that if the situation were reversed, he would come or die trying. Because of his absolute faith, not just in his brother, but in the power of love itself, he found strength, had the hope to stay alive – to wait for him to come.

We trust God because he has shown us and taught us love. We trust God because we know him and believe

The Gift of *Love*

that he loves us. We trust each other for the same reason. Because of our absolute faith in God's unfailing, steadfast love, we find the patience and the courage – in the hour of our greatest need – to overcome this world and to wait for him to come.

When every other reason fails,
love will find a way.
"Is that you, Lord?"
"Yes, John."
"*I knew you'd come –*
I've been waiting."

reflections . . .

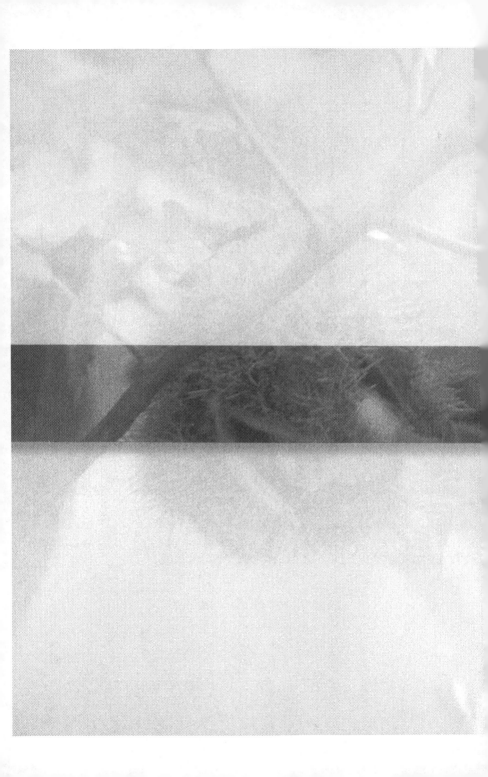

Every Good and
Perfect Gift

Don't mislabel good things that happen to you as mere "coincidence." See my divine hand in every good and perfect gift that comes your way.

Love,

Your Father of
Heavenly Lights

—FROM JAMES 1:17

At the moment your pain began, God heard your cry and began to respond. But you must stay alert, or you may mistake the work of the divine healer for mere coincidence.

A knock on your door by a friend, a letter from a loved one, a call from a concerned neighbor, an encouraging word from a family member – all of these are so much more than mere touches of human kindness. In reality, they are gifts from God.

He knows what you're going through. He's intimately familiar with pain. You see, he suffered loss, rejection, failed relationships, and crushing cruelty through the life and death of his only Son.

God's rich compassion is like an

endless stream that brings refreshment
and renewal to his beloved children. As
you yield yourself to his will, he will work
his divine providence to refresh and heal your
broken heart.

So the next time something or someone comes
along "just at the right time" to give comfort or
courage, remember that it's more than mere coincidence. The book of James reminds us that
"every good and perfect gift is from above, coming down from the Father of heavenly lights."

He knows what you need even before
you ask – even before you know what to
ask for.

God doesn't just *patch*——He renews.

God doesn't just salve sins—He *saves*.

God doesn't just *reform*——

He *transforms* men by His power.

——*Merrill C. Tenney*

I went to their rooms – pinned the notes to their doors – and left. I haven't run from many things in my life – but I ran from this one.

A Good Gift

Have you ever received a surprise gift? Something you never would have thought to ask for, something you couldn't possibly plan for. Sometimes these surprise gifts catch you off guard, and if you're not careful, you may not even realize how special they are and so miss much of the blessing.

I took my last two children to Lubbock, Texas, for college. It's a thousand miles from Montgomery to Lubbock. One was a senior but had never been away from home. The other, a freshman – our baby – the last. The last one is like the first one – but different too. It's a thousand miles from Montgomery to Lubbock.

Every Good and *Perfect Gift*

My excuse for going was that I needed to haul their stuff – which was enough to fill at least one freight car. But it was more than that – I wanted to hang on to them – even for just two or three more days. I was buying time. The inevitable good-bye was a constant oppression.

We arrived Monday afternoon, and they got settled in their rooms. On Tuesday evening, I told them I would pick them up at 8:30 Wednesday morning to help them start registration, then I was going to head home. I couldn't sleep Tuesday night, so I got up and wrote each of them a note. I went in the darkness to their rooms – pinned the notes to their doors – and left. I haven't run from many things in my life – there were many things I should have run from and didn't – but I ran from this one. I just couldn't do it.

Slowly – tearfully, alone – I drove away.

It's forty miles to Post from Lubbock, and before I got there, the sun had begun to rise. It doesn't rain often in West Texas. If you listen to the farmers, it rains like most folks go to church – Christmas and Easter – but it was raining when I left. For those of you not familiar with West Texas, I must explain something. West Texas is *flat*. The most conspicuous, the most striking, the most absolutely mind-boggling, eye-blinking feature of the landscape is its amazing *flatness*. You can see much of the world from West Texas. People who live there think you can see *all* of it. The names of the towns will help you understand the area. Names like Brown-field, Shallow-water, Post, Little-field, Earth, Plain-view, Level-land, White-face, Ropes-ville, Pan-handle – these are graphic names. The people who originated them were honest, God-fearing folks who wouldn't tell a lie. But back to my story!

Driving to Post, off to my left (to the east), without a single obstruction except for a few oil derricks, was a glorious sunrise – as clear, as totally unclouded as anything you might imagine. Off to my right (to the west) over fields of cotton stretching as far as your imagination will carry you, was a driving rainstorm. In between, ascending in a high arc from north to south, from horizon to horizon, was a rainbow. I want to use some adjectives, I want to say brilliant, spectacular, magnificent – but none of them will do. In fact, it was a double rainbow. One was absolutely clear, with distinct and unmistakable colors; the other, its shadow, was misty and vague. I could see both ends – from ground to ground. I stopped, got out, and just looked. I tried to take pictures, but I couldn't get all of it in the picture frame – not even with a wide-angle lens.

If I could tell you how hope rose in me at the sight of that rainbow – if I could tell you how clearly I felt God's presence – if I could put it into words, I know you would feel it too. I felt as if God, my Father, was laying his hand on my shoulder; I felt as if I heard him say, *"I know how you feel, John. I had to say good-bye to my Son too. It nearly broke my heart. When I saw your pain this morning, I thought you might like this little 'going away' present – from me to you. Lots of other folks will enjoy it, but really, I made it just for you."*

And then it was gone.

One minute it was there – the next it was gone – without a trace. But it will live in my heart and mind forever.

What an insight into the nature of divine fatherhood, and what an example for earthly fathers.

My children awoke that morning fully expecting me to be there; instead they found notes. I believe my absence

conveyed more than my presence could have. I believe my simple note of love and understanding communicated in a far more lasting way my feeling for them. God responded to my prayers with a totally unexpected token of love and assurance. I had prayed for strength, for faith, and assurance – and he answered my prayer in the shape of a rainbow.

I wonder how many times I have asked for healing and missed the medicine. I wonder how many times I have pouted and doubted because I thought he didn't care, when the problem was with my eyes, my ears, my heart.

"If you, then, though you are evil,
know how to give good gifts to your children,
how much more will your Father in heaven
give good gifts to those who ask him!"
—*Matthew 7:11*

reflections . . .

Printed in the United States
By Bookmasters